"Even Monkeys Fall from Trees"
and Other Japanese Proverbs

DATE DUE

APR 26 '98	

日本の諺

"Even Monkeys Fall from Trees"

and Other Japanese Proverbs

compiled and translated by David Galef
illustrations by Jun Hashimoto

with a Foreword
by Edward G. Seidensticker

Charles E. Tuttle Company
Rutland · Vermont   Tokyo · Japan

Published by the Charles E. Tuttle Company, Inc.
of Rutland, Vermont & Tokyo, Japan
with editorial offices at
Suido 1-chome, 2-6, Bunkyo-ku, Tokyo

© 1987 by Charles E. Tuttle Company

Library of Congress Catalog Card No. 87-50166
International Standard Book No. 0-8048-1625-5

First printing, 1987
Sixth printing, 1991

Printed in Japan

Table of Contents

Foreword

by Edward G. Seidensticker

The primary definition of "proverb" in the *Oxford English Dictionary* is very careful: "A short pithy saying in common and recognized use; a concise sentence, often metaphorical or alliterative in form, which is held to express some truth ascertained by experience or observation and familiar to all; an adage, a wise saw."

The three words before "express" follow the advice of *Atama kakushite shiri kakusazu* (English equivalent: "Protect yourself at all points"): foresee challenges and attacks and take measure against them. If the Oxford did as the small desk dictionaries I have with me do, and dispensed with the qualification, then the definition would be in error. Sometimes proverbs fly in the face of "experience or observation," and sometimes a proverb will contradict another one. *Kyō no yume, Ōsaka no yume* (no. 50) is vague and subject to several interpretations, some not completely in accord with common sense. Several proverbs advising caution are contradicted by *Koketsu ni irazumba koji o ezu* (no. 88), urging us to trespass upon a tigress's den.

Proverbs are what people are always saying. In this they are akin to clichés, but they are different from clichés in that they have a touch of poetry. They make lively use of imagery and they are sensitive to the music of language. They say the things that people think important in ways that people remember. They express common concerns. So a collection of proverbs is a compact treatise on the values of culture. Matching sets of proverbs from two cultures make a treatise in comparative sociology, or cultural anthropology.

It need not surprise us, though it should interest us, that the same proverbs are to be found in very different cultures. The lot of the human race is similar the world over. That not all the proverbs of one culture are to be found in another need not surprise us either, and it should interest us very much. It demonstrates that the concerns of the two are not identical. It ought to shake us a little from our parochialism.

Inevitably, Mr. Galef does not always find perfect English matches for his Japanese proverbs. Some of his equivalents do not sound like proverbs, and some do not seem precisely equivalent. He makes note in his Preface of an excellent example, the one about the nail that sticks out (no. 43). "Don't make waves" is ingenious, but it seems more an injunction to moderation than to conformity. The heart of the matter is that Americans, for example, are not exhorted by their proverbs to conform as Japanese are, so the quest for a perfect equivalent is probably doomed from the outset. It would be hard to find Japanese equivalents for some of the more puritanical of Anglo-American proverbs ("Spare the rod and spoil the child"), and Mr. Galef has perhaps not been entirely successful in finding an English equivalent for a very Buddhist one, *Ko wa sangai no kubikase* (no. 76), also about children.

I do not mean to reprove him. He has

done his work well, as has his illustrator, Mr. Hashimoto. These little frustrations are, as I have said, inevitable, and they make the book more interesting. It is a likeable book, and it tells us much about Japan.

Preface

One of the best ways to understand a culture is to examine the way its people think. Nowhere is this more evident than in a country's proverbs, wisdom distilled over centuries into epigrammatic sayings, ways of conducting one's life. From the proverb *Deru kugi wa utareru* (The protruding nail will be hammered), one can perhaps learn more about the Japanese tendency toward conformity than from a closely written text.

Many Japanese proverbs came from the Chinese centuries ago, and in more modern days sayings from Western cultures have traveled to the Orient. But the Japanese are masters at adapting, and what may have sounded Confucian two thousand years ago sounds quintessentially Japanese today. Despite modernization, Japan retains much of the world of nature in its life. Japanese proverbs, or *kotowaza*, show this debt frequently in their references to fish, trees, insects, and so on. *Kaeru no ko wa kaeru* (The child of a frog is a frog) is just one of myriad examples. And because the proverbs appear in naturalistic images, they are particularly good for easy recall and illustration. *Karuta*, a traditional card game still played by Japanese children, links proverbs with their associated pictures. The Japanese, it seems, are quite fond of their proverbs and take care to pass them on.

The origin of this book stems from a weekly column I wrote for a Japanese-English newspaper. The column was devoted mostly to *kotowaza*: the proverbs themselves and their literal translations, with perhaps a little background for support. Soon after the column's inception, I took to adding Western equivalents, partly to explain and also to help bridge the cultural gap. *Kon'ya no shirobakama* (Dyers wear undyed trousers), for example, could be rendered as the English "Shoemakers' children go barefoot." That is, provided you happened to know the English equivalent and had a good head for that sort of thing—it became a kind of game. Still, I felt continually that something was missing. In attempting to describe the meaning of *Uma no mimi ni nembutsu* (A sutra in a horse's ear), I realized what it was I wanted: a slightly bored horse, perhaps wearing a sun-hat, being lectured to by a patient priest—in a word, illustrations. Having assembled one hundred representative proverbs, I was then fortunate to find the right illustrator, Jun Hashimoto. Mr. Hashimoto represents that rare breed of talent, an artist who is also an illustrator, who could change my English translations into the far more universal language of images. The original sketch-idea for each proverb was mine, but Mr. Hashimoto inevitably came up with some of his own.

For each proverb in this book, then, there is, in addition to Mr. Hashimoto's illustrations and calligraphy, the proverb in romanized Japanese and a literal English translation. A handy list repeats the proverb and romanization, and gives an English proverb equivalent.

There were a few problems along the way worth mentioning. First, some proverbs remain slightly unclear. In a few instances, the Japanese themselves may find the sayings slightly archaic. Where obscurity is redeemed by an effective image, I have let the objection pass. Then, too, certain proverbs do not translate well or offer no clear-cut English equivalent. Others offer two or more. *Itadaku mono wa natsu de mo kosode* (A padded jacket is an acceptable gift even in summer): does that come across best as "Don't look a gift-horse in the mouth" or "It's the thought that counts"? The first involves suspicion, referring to the old practice of inspecting a horse's teeth to see how old he is. The second is closer to the spirit of the original but sounds too much like a greeting card. In general, I opted for the sound of folklore. Readers, no doubt, will disagree over the correctness of certain equivalents.

This is not the place to record all the debts I have incurred during the making of this book, or rather, it is the place, but there isn't room enough. Suffice it to list several individuals who have donated their time and intelligence: Charles Inouye, Seth Masters, Miki Inagaki, Dena Schutzer, and Edward Seidensticker. *Masaka no toki no tomo ga shin no tomo*: A friend in need is a friend indeed.

The Proverbs

1

Mago ni mo ishō.

Even a packhorse driver
looks fine in proper dress.

馬子にも衣裳

日本の諺

2

*Hiza tomo
dangō.*

**Consult anyone,
even your knees.**

日本の諺

3

Saru mo
ki kara ochiru.

Even monkeys
fall from trees.

猿も木から落ちる

日本の諺

4

*Kon'ya no
shiro-bakama.*

Dyers wear
undyed trousers.

紺屋の白袴

5

*Sen-ri no
michi mo
ippo kara.*

**Even a thousand-mile journey
begins with the first step.**

千里の道も一歩から～

6

Kani wa
kōra ni nisete
ana o horu.

Crabs dig holes according to
the size of their shells.

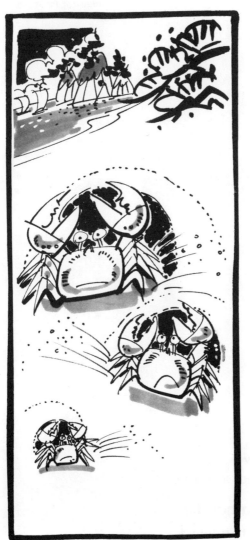

蟹は甲羅に似せて穴を掘る

7

Jinsei wa
fūzen no tomoshibi.

Life is a candle
before the wind.

人生は風前の灯

8

*Ja no michi wa
hebi.*

**Snakes follow
the way of serpents.**

蛇の道はへび

日本の諺

9

*Itadaku mono wa
natsu de mo kosode.*

A padded jacket
is an acceptable gift
even in summer.

戴くものは夏でも小袖

10

*Dōbyō
ai-awaremu.*

People with the same disease
share sympathy.

同病相憐む

11

*Hotoke no
kao mo san-do.*

**A Buddha's face
when asked three times.**

仏の顔も三度

日本の諺

12

Ichi-mon oshimi no
hyaku-zon.

One coin saved,
a hundred losses.

文惜しみの百首

日本の諺

—

13

—

Akuji
sen-ri o hashiru.

An evil act
runs a thousand miles.

悪事千里を走る

14

*Gō ni itte wa
gō ni shitagae.*

Obey the customs
of the village you enter.

郷に入っては郷に従え

15

*Hatake kara
hamaguri wa torenu.*

**You can't get clams
from a field.**

畑から蛤はとれぬ

16

Sendō ōku shite
fune yama ni noboru.

Too many boatmen
will bring a boat up a mountain.

船頭多くして船山に登る

日本の諺

17

Ura ni wa
ura ga aru.

The reverse side
has its reverse side.

一裏には裏がある。

18

*Tagei wa
mugei.*

Too many accomplishments
make no accomplishment.

多芸は無芸

日本の諺

19

Kuchi wa
wazawai no moto.

The mouth is
the cause of calamity.

口は禍いの元

20

Rakka
eda ni kaerazu,
hakyō futatabi terasazu.

Fallen blossoms
do not return to branches;
a broken mirror
does not again reflect.

落花枝に帰らず
破鏡再び照らさず

21

Oni no nyōbō
kijin ga naru.

The wife of a devil
grows worse than her mate.

鬼の女房鬼神がなる

22

Tamago to
chikai wa
kudake-yasui.

Eggs and vows
are easily broken.

卵と誓いははかせやすい

23

*Ippai wa
hito sake o nomi, ni-hai wa
sake sake o nomi, sam-bai wa
sake hito o nomu.*

**First the man takes a drink,
then the drink takes a drink,
then the drink takes the man.**

一杯は人酒を飲み　二杯は酒酒を飲み　三杯は酒人を飲む

日本の夢

24

Miso no
miso-kusai wa
jō-miso ni arazu.

The bean paste
that smells like bean paste
is not the best quality.

味噌日の味噌臭いは上噌にあらず

25

*Issun no
mushi ni mo
go-bu no tamashii.*

Even a one-inch insect
has a half-inch soul.

一寸の虫にも五分の魂

26

*Ke-bukai mono wa
iro-bukai.*

A hairy person is sexy.

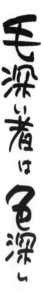

毛深い者は色深い

27

*Mochi wa
mochiya.*

**For rice cakes,
go to the rice-cake maker.**

餅は餅屋

28

Toranu tanuki no
kawa-zan'yō.

Don't estimate
the value of a badger skin
before catching the badger.

捕らぬ狸の皮算用

29

*Naku ko to
jitō ni wa
katenu.*

It is impossible
to win over a crying child
or government officials.

泣く子と地頭には勝てぬ

30

Inu mo arukeba
bō ni ataru.

A dog that walks around
will find a stick.

犬も歩けば棒にあたる

31

Hana yori
dango.

Dumplings are better
than flowers.

花より団子

団子

日本の諺

32

*Chiri mo
tsumoreba
yama to naru.*

**Even dust amassed
will grow into a mountain.**

塵を積もれば山となる

日本の諺

33

Nakittsura ni hachi.

A bee stinging a crying face.

泣き面に蜂

34

*Muri ga tōreba
dōri hikkomu.*

When illogic prevails,
reason gives way.

無理が通れば道理引っ込む

35

*Kusai mono ni
futa.*

Put a lid
on what smells bad.

夢に出る

日本の諺

36

Bimbō
hima nashi.

Poor people
have no leisure.

貧乏暇なし

37

*Se ni
hara wa
kaerarenu.*

The back
cannot take the place
of the belly.

背に腹はかえられぬ

38

Yabu o
tsutsuite
hebi o dasu.

By poking at a bamboo thicket,
one drives out a snake.

たけのこをとりました。

39

*Shitashiki
naka ni mo
reigi ari.*

There are formalities
between the closest of friends.

親しき仲にも礼儀あり

40

Inu no kenka ni
kodomo ga de,
kodomo no kenka ni
oya ga deru.

Dogfights draw children;
children's fights draw parents.

犬の喧嘩に子供がよる

子供の喧嘩に親がよる。

41

*E ni kaita
mochi wa
kuenu.*

You can't eat the rice cake
in a picture.

絵に描いた餅は食えぬ

42

Kaeru no ko wa kaeru.

The child of a frog is a frog.

蛙の子は蛙

43

Deru kugi wa
utareru.

The protruding nail
will be hammered.

出る釘は甘んじる

日本の諺

44

*Baka mo
ichi-gei.*

**Even a fool
has one talent.**

馬鹿も一芸

日本の諺

45

Makeru ga
kachi.

To lose is to win.

夏休みの少年たち

日本の諺

46

---

*Jū-nin
to-iro.*

Ten men, ten tastes.

十人十色

日本の諺

47

*Saru mono wa
hibi ni utoshi.*

Those who depart
are forgotten, day by day.

富める者は日々に疎し

日本の諺

48

Jishin,
kaminari,
kaji, oyaji.

Earthquakes, thunderbolts,
fires, fathers.

地震・雷・火事・親父

日本の諺

49

Tsume no aka o
senjite nomu.

Boil and drink
another's fingernail dirt.

爪の垢も煎じて飲む

50

Kyō no yume,
Ōsaka no yume.

Dreams in the capital,
dreams in Osaka.

尻の軽大尽の夢

51

*Tabi wa
michizure,
yo wa nasake.*

**In traveling, a companion,
in life, sympathy.**

旅は道連れ世は情け

52

He o hitte
shiri tsubome.

There is no use
scrunching up your buttocks
after a fart.

屁をひって君つぼめ

日本の諺

53

*Yoshi no zui kara
tenjō o miru.*

**One sees the sky
through a hollow reed.**

華の髄から天井を見る

54

*Mitsugo no tamashii
hyaku made.*

**The spirit
of a three year old
lasts a hundred years.**

三つ子の魂百まで

55

Monzen no kozō
narawanu kyō o yomu.

A boy
living near a Buddhist temple
can learn an untaught sutra
by heart.

門前の小僧習わぬ経を読む

海山寺

日本の諺

56

---

*Isogaba
maware.*

When in a hurry,
take the roundabout route.

名物　出前　そば

57

Nen ni wa
nen o ireyo.

Add caution to caution.

用心には 用心をいれよ

58

Uma no mimi ni nembutsu.

A sutra
in a horse's ear.

馬の耳に念仏

日本の諺

59

---

*Shiwambo no
kaki no tane.*

**A miser and
his persimmon seeds.**

呑ん坊の柿の種

60

*Atama kakushite
shiri kakusazu.*

One hides the head
and leaves the rear end
uncovered.

頭隠して尻隠さず

日本の諺

61

Zen wa isoge.

Do quickly
what is good.

善は急げ

日本の諺

62

*Toshiyori no
hiyamizu.*

An old man
dips into cold water.

全身ヨリ冷水

63

Mi kara
deta sabi.

Rust comes
from within the body.

身から出た錆

日本の諺

64

*Taigyo wa
shōchi ni
sumazu.*

**Big fish
do not live in small ponds.**

大魚は 小池に棲まず

65

Koi to
seki to wa
kakusarenu.

Love and a cough
cannot be hidden.

恋と咳とは隠されぬ

66

*Un wa
yūsha o
tasuku.*

**Fate aids
the courageous.**

風は下関を吹く

日本の諺

67

*Mukashi totta
kinezuka.*

The skill
of using a mortar and pestle
never leaves one.

昔とった杵柄

日本の諺

68

Hone ori-zon no
kutabire mōke.

Break your bones
and earn only exhaustion.

日本の諺

69

*Kahō wa
nete mate.*

**Sleep and wait
for good luck.**

果報は寝て待て

70

Yanagi no shita ni
itsu-mo
dojō wa inai.

**One cannot always find
a fish under a willow.**

柳の下にいつも鰌はいない

71

*Oite wa
ko ni shitagae.*

When you grow old,
obey your children.

老いては子に従え

72

*Nō aru taka wa
tsume o
kakusu.*

**A clever hawk
hides its claws.**

能ある鷹は爪を隠す

日本の諺

73

Chinkyaku mo
chōza ni sugireba
itowaru.

Even a welcome guest
becomes tiresome by overstaying.

珍客も長座に過れば厭われる

74

*Hachijū no
tenarai.*

One may study calligraphy
at eighty.

日本の諺

75

*Nokorimono ni
fuku ga ari.*

**The leftover piece
is lucky.**

残り物に福があり

日本の諺

76

*Ko wa
sangai no
kubikase.*

Children yoke parents
to the past, present, and future.

子は三界の首枷

日本の諺

77

Ryōyaku wa
kuchi ni
nigashi.

Good medicine
tastes bitter in the mouth.

良薬は口に苦し

78

*Kusare-nawa mo
yaku ni tatsu.*

Even a rotting rope
can be put to use.

腐れ縄も役に立つ

79

Happō bijin wa
hakujō.

An eight-sided beauty
is coldhearted.

八才美人は薄情

80

*Mi o koroshite
jin o nasu.*

One becomes virtuous
by subduing the body.

身を殺して仁をなす

日本の諺

81

Tanin no senki o
zutsū ni yamu.

**Don't get a headache
over another's lumbago.**

他人の病気を頭痛に病む

82

Yanagi ni kaze.

A willow
before the wind.

柳に風

日本の夢

83

Tanki wa sonki.

**A short temper
is a disadvantage.**

短気は損気

84

*Te ga ireba
ashi mo iru.*

**When the hand is put in,
the foot follows.**

85

*Tori naki sato no
kōmori.*

**Like a bat
in a birdless village.**

島なき里の蝙蝠

日本の諺

——

86

——

Benkei no
naki-dokoro.

The spot that makes
the warrior Benkei cry.

弁慶の泣き所

日本の諺

87

Anzuru yori
umu ga yasushi.

Childbirth is easier
than the worrying beforehand.

楽すりゃ苦がある 苦が楽し

88

Koketsu ni
irazumba
koji o ezu.

You cannot catch a tiger cub
unless you enter the tiger's den.

虎穴に入らずんば虎児を得ず

89

*Kō o
nusumu mono wa
kō ni arawaru.*

He who steals incense
smells of it.

香を聞む者は千香に現りつ

日本の夢

90

*Shōbai wa
kusa no tane.*

There are as many ways
of making a living
as seeds of grass.

商売は草の種

91

*Taishoku
hara ni mitsureba
gakumon
hara ni irazu.*

**A full belly
is not the stomach of a scholar.**

大食腹に満れば当間腹に入らず

92

*Tanshitsu
kazarazu.*

A red lacquer dish
needs no decoration.

丹
漆
飾
うら

93

*Heso o kamedomo
oyobanu.*

**It's no good
trying to bite your navel.**

膝を噛めどと及ばぬ

日本の諺

94

*Nama-byōhō wa
ō-kega no moto.*

Crude military tactics
are the cause of severe casualties.

生兵法は大怪我の元

95

*Kyō no kidaore,
Ōsaka no
kuidaore.*

Kyoto people
ruin themselves for clothing,
Osaka people for food.

京の着倒れ 大阪の食倒れ

96

*Bushi wa
kuwanedo
taka-yōji.*

**Even when a samurai has not eaten,
he holds his toothpick high.**

武士は食わねど高楊枝

日本の諺

97

Ten ni mukatte
tsuba o haku.

The spit aimed at the sky
comes back to one.

犬に向かって棒を引く

98

Kuni
horobite
sanga ari.

Destroy a country,
but its mountains and rivers
remain.

国破れて山河あり

99

*Issun saki wa
yami.*

**Darkness lies
one inch ahead.**

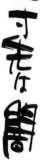

100

Nana-korobi
ya-oki.

**Fall down seven times,
get up eight.**

七転び八起き

List of Proverbs
with English Equivalents

1 馬子にも衣裳
Mago ni mo ishō.
Clothes make the man.

2 膝とも談合
Hiza tomo dangō.
Two heads are better than one.

3 猿も木から落ちる
Saru mo ki kara ochiru.
Anybody can make a mistake.

4 紺屋の白袴
Kon'ya no shiro-bakama.
Shoemakers' children go barefoot.

5 千里の道も一歩から
Sen-ri no michi mo ippo kara.
You have to start somewhere.

6 蟹は甲羅に似せて穴を掘る
Kani wa kōra ni nisete ana o horu.
Cut your coat according to your cloth.

7 人生は風前の灯
Jinsei wa fūzen no tomoshibi.
Our life is but a span.

8 蛇の道はへび
Ja no michi wa hebi.
Set a thief to catch a thief.

9 戴くものは夏でも小袖
Itadaku mono wa natsu de mo kosode.
Don't look a gift horse in the mouth.

10 同病相憐む
Dōbyō ai-awaremu.
Misery loves company.

11 仏の顔も三度
Hotoke no kao mo san-do.
To try the patience of a saint.

12 一文惜しみの百損
Ichi-mon oshimi no hyaku-zon.
Penny-wise, pound-foolish.

13 悪事千里を走る
Akuji sen-ri o hashiru.
Bad news travels fast.

14 郷に入っては郷に従え
Gō ni itte wa gō ni shitagae.
When in Rome, do as the Romans.

15 畑から蛤はとれぬ
Hatake kara hamaguri wa torenu.
You can't get blood from a stone.

16 船頭多くして船山に登る
Sendō ōku shite fune yama ni noboru.
Too many cooks spoil the broth.

17 裏には裏がある
Ura ni wa ura ga aru.
There are wheels within wheels.

18 多芸は無芸
Tagei wa mugei.
Jack of all trades, master of none.

19 口は禍いの元
Kuchi wa wazawai no moto.
The mouth is the gate of evil.

20 落花技に帰らず、破鏡再び照らさず
Rakka eda ni kaerazu, hakyō futatabi terasazu.
There's no use crying over spilt milk.

21 鬼の女房鬼神がなる
Oni no nyōbō kijin ga naru.
The apprentice outstrips the master.

22 卵と誓いは砕けやすい
Tamago to chikai wa kudake-yasui.
Actions speak louder than words.

23 一杯は人酒を飲み、二杯は酒酒を飲み、三杯は酒人を飲む
Ippai wa hito sake o nomi, ni-hai wa sake sake o nomi, sam-bai wa sake hito o nomu.
Wine is a mocker; strong drink is raging.

24 味噌の味噌臭いは上味噌にあらず
Miso no miso-kusai wa jō-miso ni arazu.
All that glitters is not gold.

25 一寸の虫にも五分の魂
Issun no mushi ni mo go-bu no tamashii.
Everything has its place.

26 毛深い者は色深い
Ke-bukai mono wa iro-bukai.
Bald and barren.

27 餅は餅屋
Mochi wa mochiya.
The right man for the right job.

28 捕らぬ狸の皮算用
Toranu tanuki no kawa-zan'yō.
Don't count your chickens before they're hatched.

29 泣く子と地頭には勝てぬ
Naku ko to jitō ni wa katenu.
You can't fight City Hall.

30 犬も歩けば棒にあたる
Inu mo arukeba bō ni ataru.
Never go looking for trouble.
or Seek and ye shall find.

31 花より団子
Hana yori dango.
Pudding before praise.

32 塵も積れば山となる
Chiri mo tsumoreba yama to naru.
Great oaks from little acorns grow.

33 泣っ面に蜂
Nakittsura ni hachi.
Adding insult to injury.

34 無理が通れば道理引っ込む
Muri ga tōreba dōri hikkomu.
Might makes right.

35 臭い物に蓋
Kusai mono ni futa.
Don't wash dirty linen in public.

36 貧乏暇なし
Bimbō hima nashi.
There is no rest for the weary.

37 背に腹はかえられぬ
Se ni hara wa kaerarenu.
Self-preservation is the first law of nature.

38 藪をつついて蛇を出す
Yabu o tsutsuite hebi o dasu.
Let sleeping dogs lie.

39 親しき仲にも礼儀あり
Shitashiki naka ni mo reigi ari.
Familiarity breeds contempt.

40 犬の喧嘩に子供が出、子供の喧嘩に親が出る
Inu no kenka ni kodomo ga de,

*kodomo no kenka ni
oya ga deru.*
One thing leads to another.

41 絵に描いた餅は食えぬ
E ni kaita mochi wa kuenu.
Never confuse art with life.

42 蛙の子は蛙
Kaeru no ko wa kaeru.
Like father, like son.

43 出る釘は打たれる
Deru kugi wa utareru.
Don't make waves.

44 馬鹿も一芸
Baka mo ichi-gei.
Even a broken clock is right twice a day.

45 負けるが勝ち
Makeru ga kachi.
The race is not to the swift.

46 十人十色
Jū-nin to-iro.
There is no accounting for tastes.

47 去る者は日々に疎し
Saru mono wa hibi ni utoshi.
Out of sight, out of mind.

48 地震、雷、火事、親父
Jishin, kaminari, kaji, oyaji.
Fear those greater than yourself.

49 爪の垢を煎じて飲む
Tsume no aka o senjite nomu.
Follow in someone's footsteps.

50 京の夢、大阪の夢
Kyō no yume, Ōsaka no yume.
Wishing will make it so.

51 旅は道連れ、世は情け
Tabi wa michizure, yo wa nasake.
A friend in need is a friend indeed.

52 屁をひって尻つぼめ
He o hitte shiri tsubome.
No use shutting the barn door after the horse has bolted.

53 葦の髄から天井を見る
Yoshi no zui kara tenjō o miru.
You can't see the forest for the trees.

54 三つ子の魂百まで
Mitsugo no tamashii hyaku made.
The child is the father of the man.

55 門前の小僧習わぬ経を読む
Monzen no kozō narawanu kyō o yomu.
Experience is the best teacher.

56 急がば回れ
Isogaba maware.
The more haste, the less speed.

57 念には念を入れよ
Nen ni wa nen o ireyo.
Look before you leap.

58 馬の耳に念仏
Uma no mimi ni nembutsu.
Preaching to deaf ears.

59 吝ん坊の柿の種
Shiwambō no kaki no tane.
A penny pincher will pick up anything.

60 頭隠して尻隠さず
Atama kakushite shiri kakusazu.
Protect yourself at all points.

61 善は急げ

Zen wa isoge.
Strike while the iron is hot.

62 年寄の冷水
Toshiyori no hiyamizu.
There's no fool like an old fool.

63 身から出た錆
Mi kara deta sabi.
As you make your bed, so you must lie in it.

64 大魚は小池に棲まず
Taigyo wa shōchi ni sumazu.
A great ship must have deep water.

65 恋と咳とは隠されぬ
Koi to seki to wa kakusarenu.
Love conquers all.

66 運は勇者を助く
Un wa yūsha o tasuku.
Fortune favors the brave.

67 昔とった杵柄
Mukashi totta kinezuka.
You never forget your own trade.

68 骨折り損のくたびれ儲け
Hone ori-zon no kutabire mōke.
Much pain, little gain.

69 果報は寝て待て
Kahō wa nete mate.
Everything comes to him who waits.

70 柳の下にいつも鰌はいない
Yanagi no shita ni itsu-mo dojō wa inai.
No one's luck lasts forever.

71 老いては子に従え
Oite wa ko ni shitagae.
The old generation must make way for the new.

72 能ある鷹は爪を隠す
Nō aru taka wa tsume o kakusu.
He who knows most speaks least.

73 珍客も長座に過れば厭わる
Chinkyaku mo chōza ni sugireba itowaru.
Fish and visitors stink in three days.

74 八十の手習い
Hachijū no tenarai.
It's never too late to learn.

75 残り物に福があり
Nokorimono ni fuku ga ari.
Last but not least.

76 子は三界の首枷
Ko wa sangai no kubikase.
Children are a burden to their parents.

77 良薬は口に苦し
Ryōyaku wa kuchi ni nigashi.
Advice when most needed is least heeded.

78 腐れ縄も役に立つ
Kusare-nawa mo yaku ni tatsu.
Necessity is the mother of invention.

79 八方美人は薄情
Happō bijin wa hakujō.
Fair and fickle.

80 身を殺して仁をなす
Mi o koroshite jin o nasu.
The world, the flesh, and the devil.

81 他人の疝気を頭痛に病む
Tanin no senki o zutsū ni yamu.
Don't meddle in others' affairs.

82 柳に風
Yanagi ni kaze.
Follow the path of least resistance.

83 短気は損気
Tanki wa sonki.
Be slow to anger, quick to befriend.

84 手が入れば足も入る
Te ga ireba ashi mo iru.
Draw back while there is still time.

85 鳥なき里の蝙蝠
Tori naki sato no kōmori.
Like a one-eyed man in the kingdom of the blind.

86 弁慶の泣き所
Benkei no naki-dokoro.
Everyone has his Achilles' heel.

87 案ずるより生むが易し
Anzuru yori umu ga yasushi.
It's always darkest before the dawn.

88 虎穴に入らずんば虎子を得ず
Koketsu ni irazumba koji o ezu.
Nothing ventured, nothing gained.

89 香を盗む者は香に現わる
Kō o nusumu mono wa kō ni arawaru.
Guilt will out.

90 商売は草の種
Shōbai wa kusa no tane.
Each to his own trade.

91 大食腹に満れば学問腹に入らず
Taishoku hara ni mitsureba gakumon hara ni irazu.
Hunger sharpens the mind.

92 丹漆飾らず
Tanshitsu kazarazu.
Beauty alone is sufficient.

93 臍を嚙めども及ばぬ
Heso o kamedomo oyobanu.
Don't cut off your nose to spite your face.

94 生兵法は大怪我の元
Nama-byōhō wa ō-kega no moto.
A little learning is a dangerous thing.

95 京の着倒れ、大阪の食い倒れ
Kyō no kidaore, Ōsaka no kuidaore.
Each goes to hell in his own way.

96 武士は食わねど高楊枝
Bushi wa kuwanedo taka-yōji.
One must put on a brave display even in adversity.

97 天に向かって唾を吐く
Ten ni mukatte tsuba o haku.
Don't spit into the wind.

98 国滅びて山河あり
Kuni horobite sanga ari.
The land outlasts the king.

99 一寸先は闇
Issun saki wa yami.
No man knows his own future.

100 七転び八起き
Nana-korobi ya-oki.
If at first you don't succeed, try, try again.